RHINE RIVER (

TRAVEL GUIDE

The Updated Companion to Discover Attractive Castles and Vineyards

David A. Chris

Gratitude Page

The Rhine, a majestic artery of history, opens up before you, promising a soul-stirring voyage. We are thrilled to be your traveling companion on this wonderful adventure.

This guide is a labor of love dedicated to the Rhine's unique tapestry. We are deeply grateful to the historians and local experts who donated their invaluable knowledge, crafting a story of the region's intriguing past. A heartfelt thank you to the brilliant photographers who captured the Rhine's magnificent splendor in engaging images.

However, our deepest gratitude goes to you, the traveler. Your curiosity and wanderlust motivate our desire to create extraordinary travel experiences. With this book in hand, you'll be able to confidently travel the Rhine, discovering hidden gems and enjoying every second of your journey.

Accept the magic of the Rhine Valley. Explore the lovely towns and majestic castles. Enjoy the region's wonderful food while sipping on its famous wines. Immerse yourself in the rich tapestry of history and culture that runs through every area.

Most importantly, explore responsibly. Respect the delicate ecosystems, help local populations, and tread lightly in this magnificent landscape. Create memories that will always hold a special place in your heart, recollections linked with the Rhine's enchantment.

Thank You.

Table of Contents

Rhine River Cruise

SCAN THE QR CODE

1. Open your device's camera app.
2. Point the camera at the QR code.
3. Ensure the QR code is within the frame and well-lit.
4. Wait for your device to recognize the QR code.
5. Once recognized, tap on the notification or follow the prompt to access the content or action associated with the QR code.

INTRODUCTION

Imagine a tour through historic castles whispering secrets in the breeze, vineyards sprawling across emerald slopes, and lovely villages beckoning with half-timbered homes. This fascinating tapestry is the Rhine River Cruise, which unfolds like a storybook through the heart of Europe.

The Rhine, a gorgeous stream that has functioned as a trading route for millennia, runs for almost 780 miles across four countries: Switzerland, France, Germany, and the Netherlands. As you glide across its surface, expect to be immersed in a rich cultural tapestry.

Christianity is the major religion along the Rhine, with magnificent cathedrals and old churches dotting the landscape. However, the region has a diverse mix of races and faiths, reflecting its past as a crossroads of Europe.

Speaking of history, the Rhine is a living reminder of the past. From the Roman legions that first crossed its waters to the rise and fall of empires, every curve in the river tells a story about a bygone era. Majestic castles poised on cliffs like sentinels, quaint medieval towns, and the haunting echoes of stories will capture your mind.

The Euro (€) is the official currency for much of the Rhine's course. Before you begin, familiarize yourself with coins and bills. Rest assured that most businesses take credit cards, but keeping some Euros on hand is usually a smart idea for smaller purchases or local markets.

The convenience of a Rhine River Cruise is one of its most appealing features. The Schengen Agreement allows for unfettered transit between most Rhine countries, allowing you to immerse yourself in each destination's unique culture without having to deal with customs formalities.

Here's the greatest part: Rhine Valley culture is friendly and hospitable. Expect to be greeted with a smile and a slower pace of life. While English is often spoken in tourist regions, knowing a few basic German phrases will greatly enhance your trip.

So pack your bags, a sense of adventure, and this reliable guide. The Rhine River awaits, ready to reveal its majesty throughout your amazing European vacation.

CHAPTER 1

Overview of Rhine River

The Rhine River Cruise provides an experience unlike any other. As your yacht glides along the waterway, a thrilling story emerges, showcasing an area rich in history, bustling with varied cultures, and surrounded by stunning landscapes. Let us plunge into the heart of this incredible voyage, discovering the rich fabric of the Rhine's interesting past, vibrant cultures, and stunning landscapes.

History of Rhine River

The Rhine has a history as diverse and vibrant as the streams that flow through it.

Ancient Echoes: Celtic tribes were the first to murmur of human presence along the Rhine. These early colonists were followed by the Romans, who realized the river's strategic value and built cities and forts to build the framework for future trade routes.

Medieval Marvels: The Middle Ages saw the establishment of mighty kingdoms and the construction of the famous Rhine castles. These beautiful fortresses, typically placed high on cliffs overlooking the river, acted as both defensive strongholds and emblems of power. Legends such as Siegfried and the Nibelungs glorified the region, adding folklore to its historical fabric.

A Commercial Hub: As Europe emerged from the Middle Ages, the Rhine grew into an important commerce route between the North Sea and the Mediterranean. Along the banks, bustling communities emerged, excelling in crafts, winemaking, and trade. This thriving commercial activity encouraged a dynamic exchange of ideas and cultures, resulting in the region's distinct character.

Modern Metamorphosis: The Industrial Revolution brought a surge of growth on the Rhine's coasts. Major cities like Cologne and Rotterdam emerged as industrial powerhouses. Today, the Rhine remains an important economic route, as well as a popular tourist destination.

A Living Museum: Your Rhine River Cruise will serve as a daily reminder of the region's historical significance. Explore the majesty of the Cologne Cathedral, a UNESCO World Heritage Site, or marvel at the magnificent Marksburg Castle, one of the few Rhine fortifications that has survived throughout history. Each stop on your journey provides an insight into the Rhine's intriguing history.

Culture

The Rhine Valley has a complex cultural tapestry made from the threads of numerous ethnicities and customs.

German Heartbeat: The Rhine Valley experience is centered around German culture. Expect hearty cuisine, exciting events such as Oktoberfest, and a strong respect for classical music and art. Explore attractive Christmas markets, enjoy a glass of Riesling wine in a snug wine cellar, or attend a traditional open-air performance to thoroughly immerse yourself in the region's culture.

French Flair: As your voyage approaches France, a dash of Gallic flare is added to the mix. Explore the Alsatian region, known for its charming villages with half-timbered houses, and indulge in Alsatian cuisine, which includes flammekueche (a savory tart) and choucroute garnie (meat sauerkraut).

Dutch Delights: The Netherlands' renowned windmills and canals complete the cultural tapestry. Explore the dynamic metropolis of Amsterdam, noted for its creative legacy and liberal attitude, or travel to lovely Dutch towns covered with bright flowers.

While German is the primary language in the region, English is often spoken in tourist destinations. Learning a few basic German phrases, such as "Guten Tag" (Hello) and "Danke" (Thank you), will improve your experience and show respect for the local culture.

Geography and Topography of Rhine River

The Rhine River winds through a breathtakingly beautiful terrain, providing a visual feast for the eyes.

Dramatic Views: The Upper Middle Rhine Valley, a UNESCO World Heritage Site, is unquestionably the highlight of the Rhine River Cruise. Towering cliffs planted with vines and capped with historic castles form a spectacular vista. Lush trees cover the slopes, while lovely settlements nestled along the riverbed provide a touch of humanity.

Vineyard valleys: The Rhine Valley is a well-known wine region. Rolling hillsides covered in meticulously managed vines extend as far as the eye can see. Sample the region's famous Riesling wines, which are known for their crisp acidity and flowery flavors, at a conventional winery or on a wine tasting tour.

Enchanted Towns: The terrain is dotted with quaint villages with half-timbered cottages and cobblestone streets. Wander through crowded marketplaces brimming with local products and crafts, or simply relax at a riverbank cafe and take in the lovely scenery. Watch youngsters play by the water's side, listen to the calm murmur of the river, and take in the fresh air - the ideal respite from the hurry and bustle of daily life.

Majestic River Capes: The Rhine itself is a stunning site to behold. Watch barges delivering products slowly navigate the waterway, demonstrating the river's continued function as a trading route. Watch birds soar overhead, their songs echoing off the cliffs, and watch the ever-changing play of light on the water's surface. As the sun sets, spreading a warm warmth over the surrounding area, the Rhine changes into a sight straight out of a fairytale.

Beyond the Riverbank: Go beyond the river to discover hidden gems. Hike through lush woodlands along old pathways that weave around the hills. Explore lovely countryside communities that have been undisturbed by time and where traditions are fiercely protected. For an adrenaline rush, pedal along designated paths that provide breathtaking views of the Rhine Valley from a new angle.

The Rhine River Cruise is an amazing experience that combines history, culture, and stunning beauty into a compelling tapestry. So pack your bags, a sense of adventure, and this reliable guide. The Rhine awaits, eager to work its charm throughout your wonderful European holiday.

CHAPTER 2

Planning Your Trip

The Rhine River Cruise entices with its promise of beautiful scenery, fascinating history, and dynamic cultures. However, before setting sail, some necessary preparation is required. This section will walk you through all you need to know to have a seamless and memorable experience.

Best Time to Visit

The best time for your Rhine River Cruise is determined by your unique preferences and desired experiences. Here's a summary of the seasons and their offerings:

Spring (April-May): The Rhine Valley bursts with color. Wildflowers bloom on the slopes, vineyards emerge from their winter slumber, and the weather is bright and pleasant. Crowds are typically lower than during peak season, and you may be able to locate some great cruise discounts. However, some excursions and attractions may not be completely operating yet.

Summer (June-August) brings sunshine, longer days, and a lively mood to the Rhine Valley. This is peak season, so expect increased crowds and prices. However, you will get access to all of the region's excursions, festivals, and events. The weather is great for seeing places, doing outdoor activities, and taking in the bustling ambiance.

Autumn (September-October): The Rhine Valley is painted in a stunning array of colors. Forests become a blazing tapestry of reds, oranges, and yellows, providing a stunning backdrop for your cruise. The weather continues mild, and crowds begin to drop out, resulting in a good blend of pleasant weather and manageable numbers.

Winter (November–March): The Rhine Valley is transformed into a wonderland. The snow-covered summits and frosted vineyards create a magnificent atmosphere. While certain excursions and attractions may have limited hours or be closed entirely, beautiful Christmas markets bring a touch of magic to the area. This is the quietest and most economical time to visit, ideal for a relaxing getaway.

Choosing Your Ideal Cruise: Rhine River cruises are available in a variety of lengths, itinerary options, and themes. When deciding on a pace, keep your interests in mind. Short cruises (4-5 days) concentrate on a single stretch of the river, whereas longer cruises (7-10 days) cover the full length and travel to adjacent nations. Thematic cruises may include wine sampling, Christmas markets, or historical excursions.

The Rhine Valley comes alive with lively festivities all year. Look into upcoming events that overlap with your vacation dates to add an added layer of excitement to your trip. Oktoberfest, with its loud celebrations and traditional beer, has a global appeal, but there are numerous smaller, more local festivals that provide a distinct cultural experience.

Weather

Packing for your Rhine River Cruise is determined by the season you select to visit. However, some general standards will ensure you're ready for anything.

Pack layers for the spring and autumn seasons! The weather can be variable, with cool mornings and evenings followed by scorching afternoons. Bring a lightweight rain jacket and comfortable walking shoes.

Summer: Pack breathable textiles such as cotton and linen. Sunscreen, a hat, and sunglasses are necessary. You might also want to bring a light sweater for evenings, which can be cool.

Winter: Bring warm clothes! The Rhine Valley may get rather cold in the winter. Thermal layers, a thick coat, waterproof boots, a cap, and gloves are required.

Comfortable walking shoes are essential for exploring towns and villages, regardless of season. A good camera is required to capture the beautiful countryside and lovely towns. Bring a reusable water bottle to remain hydrated while avoiding single-use plastics. If you are traveling from a nation that has a different electrical system, you will need an adaptor plug.

How to Get there

The Rhine Valley region is served by several major airports, including Frankfurt Airport (Germany), Amsterdam Airport Schiphol (Netherlands), and Zurich Airport. Depending on your cruise operator and itinerary, you could embark in any city along the river. Check your cruise specifics for precise arrival information.

Train Travel: The Rhine Valley is easily accessible because of Europe's efficient rail network. Major cities such as Cologne, Frankfurt, and Amsterdam are well served by high-speed trains. Once you arrive at your embarkation location, your cruise line will normally arrange transfers to the cruise port for you.

While your cruise will provide transportation along the river, visiting the cities and villages on your own requires more planning. Many towns are pedestrian-friendly, so walking is the ideal way to explore. Alternatively, you can rent bicycles for a more active excursion, providing beautiful vistas from a different angle. Some larger towns may have public transit options, such as buses or trams. Taxis are widely available in most major cities and tourist destinations.

Visa and Entry Requirements

Visa Considerations: Most travelers from the United States, Canada, Australia, and New Zealand do not need a visa to enter the Rhine countries (Germany, France, the Netherlands, and Switzerland) for stays of less than 90 days. However, it is critical to double-check visa requirements with your home nation's embassy or consulate well in advance, particularly if you intend to extend your stay or travel from another country.

Passport Power: Make sure your passport is valid for at least six months after your anticipated return date from Europe. Having a few blank pages for entry stamps is also advisable. Make duplicates of your passport's photo and information page and store them separate in case it is lost or stolen.

Travel Insurance: Purchasing travel insurance is strongly advised. It can give you peace of mind in the event of unforeseen situations such as travel cancellations, medical problems, or misplaced luggage.

Currency Exchange: The Euro (€) is the official currency for the majority of the Rhine River Cruise. Before you leave, exchange some money into Euros for little purchases or circumstances where credit cards may not be accepted. Many ATMs are located in major towns and cities along the river, allowing you to withdraw money throughout your journey.

Most mobile phone companies offer easily accessible international roaming services, making it simple to stay in touch with loved ones back home. Alternatively, try acquiring a local SIM card for your phone upon arrival, which can be a less expensive method to stay connected. Most cafes, restaurants, and hotels provide Wi-Fi connection, allowing you to stay connected on social media and check your emails.

With careful planning and this guide by your side, you'll be on your way to a memorable Rhine River cruise. Now, let's dive into the thrilling world of onboard experiences and shore excursions that await you!

CHAPTER 3

Must-See Attractions

The Rhine River, a historical tapestry woven through beautiful landscapes, is full of wonders that wait to be discovered. This section focuses on ten notable landmarks that embody the region's magic:

Cologne Cathedral

This massive Gothic cathedral, which had been under construction for nearly 500 years before its completion in 1880, is undoubtedly Germany's most well-known religious structure, with two massive towers that serve as the defining icon of Cologne's skyline.

Lorelei Rock

Loreley Rock is located in the Upper Middle Rhine Valley, a UNESCO-listed part of the Rhine River that runs 40 miles (65 kilometers) between Koblenz and Bingen. This narrow stretch of the river was notorious for hazardous rapids, which could explain the shipwrecking siren legends. To visit, take a Rhine riverboat tour—from one-day excursions to multi-day journeys—many of which pass by

Loreley Rock. The brave can hike to the summit for river views.

Marksburg Castle

Marksburg is an excellent example of a medieval fortification. Originally built by the Rhine's strong Eppstein family, it saw the erection of many Gothic buildings in the 1300s, giving it its current form, before being extended into a fortress in the 1400s and utilized as a jail in the 1800s.

In-house castle tours are the sole way for visitors to explore Marksburg. These take you through its features, including the Great Hall, kitchen, armory, cannon-guarded walls overlooking the Rhine, and stables, which house a medieval torture museum. Many visitors choose to see Marksburg exclusively from the outside on boat journeys from Koblenz to Mainz, Boppard, or Rudesheim, while others take day-long cruises that land at Braubach. Marksburg is also a destination on multi-day Rhine cruises departing from locations such as Koblenz and Bonn.

Heidelberg Castle

Heidelberg Castle is one of the most famous castle ruins in the world. From here, you have an outstanding view of the town, including its stunning buildings, the Alte Brücke bridge, and the tranquil Neckar.

Its history has been active since its building began in the thirteenth century. Over three centuries, the castle's lords proceeded to expand the structure. As a result, the castle has architectural evidence from the Gothic and Renaissance periods, namely when the castle was at its peak, such as the Ottheinrich building, one of Germany's most exquisite Renaissance palaces. After being destroyed during the Palatinate War of Succession, the castle was never fully restored. It gradually deteriorated before resurging during the Romantic period.

Schloss Benrath

Schloss Benrath is located in the south of Düsseldorf. Architect Nicolas de Pigage designed the latter, which is regarded as one of Europe's most stunning late Baroque garden palaces. The remarkably well-preserved architectural complex, which includes a main structure, eastern and western cavalier wings, two gatehouses, and four guardhouses, provides a detailed look at courtly life in the second half of the 18th century. Nicolas de Pigage also planned the park that flanks the Rhine embankment. The Museum of Garden Art, a one-of-a-kind collection worldwide, takes visitors on a trip through centuries of European garden art and the history of the Benrath Palace.

Königsallee

No street better exemplifies the city's affluence than Knigstrasse, which is lined with luxury shops and restaurants.

Rhine Gorge

The Rhine Gorge is located just beyond the gates of the Alpine City of Chur and is easily accessible via public transportation. What began as the Flims landslide has evolved into a unique natural backdrop: 10,000 years ago, 10 billion cubic meters of rock thundered into the valley. Since then, the Rhine has cut a passage through the bedrock between Ilanz and Reichenau. The end consequence is a ravine aptly named the Swiss Grand Canyon. The strange stone formations surrounded by pine trees entice rail travelers, ramblers, mountain bikers, and river rafts from all over the world. Several panoramic platforms along the valley provide stunning views of the Rhine valley, known as "Ruinaulta" in Romansh.

Moselle

The Moselle, often called as d'Musel by Luxembourgers, is located in the east of Luxembourg. The region is named after the river that forms the Grand Duchy's 42-kilometer natural boundary with Germany. Rather than building fences, this tranquil watercourse represents a unity space with the next countries. It also symbolizes the openness of a region that witnessed the signing of a vital instrument in Europe's development: the Schengen Agreement.

The Moselle Valley, with its comparatively mild climate, is largely a wine-growing region with a long history. This land of flavors encourages relaxation: hikes through vineyards, boat or bike tours, wellness circuits, and wine-growing villages welcome you all year. Do not miss the next grape and wine festivals, and bask in the Moselle sun just 20 kilometers from Luxembourg City!

Gutenberg Museum

This museum, located in Johannes Gutenberg's hometown, features a recreation of his original printing press as well as a variety of other exhibits.

Altstadt

The Old Town of Heidelberg begins at Sofienstrasse and leads to the castle. In the center is the University Area (Germany's oldest university), the main commercial strip (Hauptstrasse), and the iconic Karl-Theodor-Bridge / Old Bridge.

CHAPTER 4

Practical Tips and Guidelines

The Rhine River Cruise's allure extends beyond its breathtaking scenery and historical attractions. A smooth and enjoyable trip is dependent on being prepared and having the necessary information at your fingertips. This section provides you with practical suggestions and guidelines to ensure that your Rhine River Cruise goes smoothly.

What to Pack

Packing for your Rhine River Cruise varies depending on the season, but some general necessities will ensure you're ready for anything:

Clothing

Spring and Autumn: Bring layers because the weather can be unpredictable, with cool mornings and evenings giving place to pleasant afternoons. Bring a lightweight rain jacket and comfortable walking shoes.

Summer: Choose breathable textiles like cotton and linen. Pack sunscreen, a hat, and sunglasses. Include a light sweater for chilly evenings.

Winter: Bring warm clothes; the Rhine Valley can be chilly. Thermal layers, a thick coat, waterproof boots, hats, and gloves are required.

Footwear: Comfortable walking shoes are essential for exploring towns and villages. Pack sandals or lightweight shoes for resting on the deck or in warm weather.

Essentials

- A good camera to capture the breathtaking scenery and little towns.
- A reusable water bottle can help you remain hydrated while avoiding single-use plastics.
- If you're traveling from a nation with a different electrical system, bring an adapter plug.
- drugs - Bring adequate prescription drugs for the entire trip, along with a doctor's note if necessary. Include common over-the-counter medications such as pain relievers, allergy meds, and digestive aids.

Optional extras:

- Binoculars for birdwatching or admiring the view from the sundeck.
- A little umbrella for unexpected rain.

- A guidebook or phrasebook for the area to help you explore.
- A tiny daypack to carry essentials on seaside trips.

Check with your cruise line about laundry service availability onboard. Pack accordingly, knowing that you can refresh your clothes as needed.

Safety Precautions

Important Precautions for Your Rhine River Cruise

The Rhine Valley is typically safe, however basic precautions are always recommended:

Be mindful of your surroundings: Keep a watch on your belongings, particularly in crowded situations.

Respect local customs: When visiting religious sites, dress modestly and avoid taking photographs were banned.

Stay hydrated: Especially in hot weather, drink plenty of water throughout your journey.

Sun Safety: Use sunscreen on a daily basis, particularly during high sun hours. Wear a cap and sunglasses to provide extra protection.

Emergency Preparedness: Learn about your cruise ship's emergency procedures. Locate the life jackets and muster stations.

Medical Concerns: Look up any immunizations or health cautions suggested for the places you'll be visiting.

Getting travel insurance is strongly advised. It can give you peace of mind in the event of unforeseen situations such as travel cancellations, medical problems, or misplaced luggage. Choose a plan that is appropriate for your requirements and budget.

Transportation Options

Cruise ships are typically straightforward to navigate. Deck plans are easily available, and crew members are always eager to help with directions. Elevators are generally provided for individuals who require them.

Shore Excursions: Most cruise companies provide a wide range of shore excursions for seeing communities, visiting historical sites, and participating in local activities. These excursions provide an easy way to explore while your cruise handles transportation logistics. Alternatively, you can explore individually.

strolling: Since many towns are pedestrian-friendly, strolling is the greatest way to explore.

Bicycle Rentals: Rent a bicycle for a more active excursion that provides spectacular vistas from a different angle.

Some larger towns may have public transit options, such as buses or trams.

Taxis: Taxis are widely available in most major cities and tourist destinations.

Currency and Payment

The Euro (€) is the official currency for much of the Rhine River Cruise (Germany, France, and the Netherlands). Here's how to run your funds smoothly:

Money Exchange: Before you leave, convert some money to Euros for little purchases or circumstances where credit cards may not be accepted.

ATMs: There are numerous ATMs located in major towns and cities along the river, allowing you to withdraw cash throughout your journey. Be mindful of any fees for overseas ATM withdrawals.

Credit Cards: Credit cards are generally accepted in most tourist destinations and on cruise ships. However, notify your credit card company of your travel plans to avoid any problems with potential fraud warnings. Consider utilizing a credit card that offers travel incentives or benefits, such as travel insurance.

Tipping: The proper way to leave a tip changes a little from country to country, but in general, tipping for good service is appreciated. Check with your cruise line about their tipping policies onboard. It is common to leave a little gratuity for good service on shore excursions and restaurants.

Travel Insurance

Travel insurance is strongly advised for your Rhine River Cruise. It can provide financial security and peace of mind in the event of unanticipated situations. Here's what you should consider:

Coverage Alternatives: Travel insurance provides protection against a multitude of circumstances, encompassing medical-related cancellations or interruptions, inclement weather, and domestic and international unrest. It can also protect against lost luggage, medical crises, and travel delays.

Choosing a Plan: Choose a plan that fits your demands and budget. Consider the length of your trip, the value of your travel investment (cruise fare, flights, etc.), and your own risk tolerance.

Before acquiring travel insurance, carefully understand the terms and restrictions. Understand what is and is not covered, and pay special attention to any exceptions or limitations.

Following these practical advice and instructions will prepare you to manage the Rhine River Cruise with confidence and ease. Now, let's dive into the thrilling world of onboard experiences and enticing shore excursions that await you!

CHAPTER 5

Historical Culture

The Rhine River Cruise immerses you in a region rich in history, folklore, and culinary traditions. This section digs into the Rhine's rich tapestry, revealing intriguing stories, legends, and tasty pleasures that await you on your voyage.

Rhine River History

The Rhine has a history as vibrant and enriching as the streams that flow through it.

Ancient Echoes: Celtic tribes were the first to murmur of human presence along the Rhine. These early occupants paved the way for succeeding towns and trade routes, eventually giving way to the Romans, who realized the river's strategic value. Roman outposts and forts paved the way for prospering communities along the riverbanks.

Medieval Marvels: The Middle Ages saw the establishment of mighty kingdoms and the construction of the famous Rhine castles. These beautiful fortresses, typically placed high on cliffs overlooking the river, acted as both defensive strongholds and emblems of power. From the majestic Marksburg Castle, which has survived amazingly well, to the fabled ruins of Rheinstein, each castle tells a story of knights, chivalry, and epic wars.

A Commercial Hub: As Europe emerged from the Middle Ages, the Rhine grew into an important commerce route between the North Sea and the Mediterranean. Along the banks, bustling communities such as Cologne sprung up, excelling in crafts, winemaking, and trade. This thriving commercial activity encouraged a dynamic exchange of ideas and cultures, resulting in the region's distinct character. Explore Cologne's beautiful Gothic cathedral, a witness to the affluent age.

Modern Metamorphosis: The Industrial Revolution brought a surge of growth on the Rhine's coasts. Major cities like Cologne and Rotterdam emerged as industrial powerhouses. Today, the Rhine remains an important waterway for trade, bringing travelers from all over the world eager to see its rich history and enchanting beauty.

Your Rhine River cruise will serve as a continual reminder of the region's historical significance.

Explore the Upper Middle Rhine Valley, a UNESCO World Heritage Site filled with magnificent castles and vineyards. Marvel at the architectural marvels of cities such as Heidelberg, which bear witness to the Renaissance period. Each stop on your journey provides an insight into the Rhine's intriguing history.

Rhine River Legends and Folklore

The Rhine Valley is rich in myths and stories, which add to the region's charm.

The Nibelungenlied: This epic poem, regarded as Germany's national epic, recounts of the hero Siegfried, his love for Kriemhild, and the Nibelungs' treasure. Many castles along the Rhine are associated with characters and events from this epic story, giving a sense of mystery to your journey.

Lorelei: The fascinating legend of Lorelei, a beautiful siren who lured sailors to their deaths on the dangerous cliffs of the Rhine Gorge, continues to attract visitors. Several locations along the river claim to be the site of her hauntings, giving an element of mystery to your tour.

Rhine Maidens: These fabled creatures, protectors of the Rhine's treasures, are thought to live deep within the river. Their visage is frequently represented in art and legend, contributing to the region's allure.

The region's history is also intertwined with real-life people and events. Learn about Roman emperors who utilized the Rhine as a frontier, Charlemagne's huge Frankish Empire, and the Rhine's significance in key historical events such as the Thirty Years' War.

Rhine River Wine Culture

The Rhine Valley is a famous wine area with a long and storied history of grape production and winemaking.

Grape Expectations: The region is best known for Riesling, a white grape variety famed for its clean acidity, floral aromas, and ability to age gracefully. Other grape varieties cultivated in the region include Pinot Noir and Spätburgunder (the German term for Pinot Noir), which provide a diverse range of flavors to explore.

Vineyard Vistas: The Rhine Valley environment is characterized by rolling hillsides covered with meticulously managed vineyards. As your cruise travels through the region, you'll be treated to stunning views of vineyards bathed in sunshine. Many vineyards provide tours and tastings, allowing you to see the winemaking process firsthand and sample the region's wonderful offerings.

Wine Festivals: Throughout the year, attractive towns and villages along the Rhine Valley host exciting wine festivals. These joyful festivities commemorate the harvest, allow attendees to sample local wines, and highlight the region's rich culinary traditions.

Rhine River Cuisine

The Rhine Valley's culinary culture goes beyond its famous wines, providing a wonderful trip for your taste senses.

substantial Fare: The region's food is noted for its substantial and filling dishes, which represent the hardworking nature of its residents. Expect to eat luscious sausages like bratwurst, slow-cooked stews like sauerbraten (marinated roast), and hearty potato dishes.

Local Specialties: Each Rhine region has its own distinct culinary delights. Try "Flammkuchen" (a savory tart) with a glass of Riesling in Alsace, "Himmel und Erde" (mashed potatoes with applesauce) in the Middle Rhine, or "Pannenkoeken" (Dutch pancakes) with fresh berries as you cruise through the Netherlands.

Fresh Flavors: Rhine Valley cuisine makes extensive use of locally available products. Freshly caught river trout and salmon, seasonal vegetables such as asparagus and cabbage, and locally produced cheeses all contribute to a delightful and authentic dining experience.

Sweet Endings: A meal is incomplete without dessert! Discover the region's delicious pastries, cakes, and chocolates. For a truly indulgent treat, try "Baumkuchen" (layered tree cake) with a cup of coffee, or a slice of "Schwarzwälder Kirschtorte" (Black Forest Cake).

The Rhine River Cruise is a sensory feast, with a riveting blend of history, mythology, and gastronomic pleasures. At each stop on your tour, you'll uncover a fresh story, a riveting legend, or a flavor that will leave you craving more. So join us on this wonderful voyage and raise a glass to the beautiful tapestry woven by the Mighty Rhine!

CHAPTER 6

Useful Resource and Contacts

A successful Rhine River Cruise depends on being prepared and having the necessary information at your fingertips. This section provides you with valuable tools and contacts to guarantee a seamless and enriching trip.

Rhine River Cruise Not to Miss

The Rhine Valley provides a wealth of views and activities. Here are some not-to-miss highlights to include on your itinerary:

UNESCO World Heritage Sites: Immerse yourself in history by visiting the Upper Middle Rhine Valley, a designated World Heritage Site. This gorgeous stretch of river is studded with enchanting castles, quaint villages, and rolling vineyards, providing a picturesque journey through time.

Iconic Rhine Castles: No Rhine River Cruise is complete without admiring the magnificent castles that border the riverfront. Marksburg Castle, one of the few remaining unconquered fortifications, provides insight into medieval life. Rheinstein

Castle, a magnificent ruin built atop a rock, offers breathtaking views of the valley below. Many castles provide tours, allowing you to explore their majestic halls while learning about their fascinating history.

Enchanting Towns and Villages: The Rhine Valley is full of lovely towns and villages, each with its own distinct character. Explore the medieval city of Cologne, known for its stunning Gothic cathedral. Wander the cobbled alleyways of Rüdesheim, a winemaking town famed for its vibrant atmosphere. Stroll around the lovely canals of Amsterdam, a city known for its cultural legacy and liberal spirit. Each town provides opportunities to explore local culture, experience regional food, and discover hidden gems.

Wine Tastings & Vineyard Explorations: Immerse yourself in the area's renowned wine culture. Many wineries throughout the Rhine Valley provide tours and tastings, allowing you to learn about the winemaking process while also enjoying the region's wonderful offerings. Explore the sweeping vineyards that cover the hillsides and find the ideal Riesling to match your Rhine River Cruise experience.

Festive Celebrations: The Rhine Valley comes alive with bright events every year. Enjoy the festive atmosphere of Oktoberfest in Munich, complete with loud music, traditional costumes, and brimming steins of beer. Immerse yourself in the romance of Christmas markets, which are decked with dazzling lights and sell unique local goods and delectable foods. Look for future events that overlap with your vacation dates to add an added layer of excitement to your trip.

Many cruise lines provide themed trips tailored to specific hobbies, such as castle exploration, wine sampling, or Christmas markets. To get the most out of your cruise, think about your preferences.

Local Phrases

Learning a few simple German words will greatly enhance your Rhine River Cruise experience. Here are some helpful Phrases to get you started:

Greetings:
Good day!
Grüß Gott (Hello) (South Germany)
Hallo (Informal)
Common Courtesy:

Bitte (Please) and Dank (Thank you).

Excuse me.

Basic Needs:

Ja (yes).

Nein (No).

Wasser (water)

Where is the toilet? (Where are the restrooms?)

Install a language translation app on your phone for on-the-go assistance with more difficult phrases or menus.

Tourist Information Centers

Tourist information centers are a wealth of knowledge and can be a helpful resource on your Rhine River Cruise. Here's what they have to offer:

Maps and Brochures: Get free maps, brochures, and guides to help you get about the towns and cities you visit.

Local advice: Ask the informed staff for advice on restaurants, sights, and hidden gems.

Event Information: Stay up to date on festivals, exhibitions, and other events taking place during your visit.

Obtain assistance navigating public transit networks in the towns and cities along the river.

Tourist information centers are typically found in rail stations, big town squares, or popular tourist destinations. Look for signs that display the international tourist information symbol (an "i" with a circle around it).

Emergency Contacts

In case of an emergency, here are some crucial contact numbers to keep handy:

Emergency Services: Call 112 for quick assistance from police, ambulance, or fire departments.

Local Police: Most municipalities' police stations will have contact information prominently displayed outside. You can also inquire at your hotel or cruise line about the local police station's phone number.

Cruise company Security: Your cruise company will have its own security professionals on board to assist you with any difficulties or concerns you may have during your voyage. They can be reached by dialing a special number from your cabin phone or going to the security office onboard.

Learn about the emergency procedures onboard your cruise ship. Locate the life jackets, muster stations, and safety signs. In the unusual case of an emergency, being cool and obeying crew instructions are critical.

With these resources and contacts at your fingertips, you'll be well-prepared to handle your Rhine River Cruise with confidence and simplicity. Set sail now and prepare to be dazzled by the magic of the Rhine!

CHAPTER 7

Preparation and Travel Kits

Going on a Rhine River Cruise is an exciting concept. To ensure a seamless and comfortable journey, precise planning is essential. This section provides you with complete advice on packing the necessities and putting together the ideal travel kit for your Rhine River adventure.

Documents

A valid passport is the most important document for your Rhine River cruise. Ensure that your passport is valid for at least six months after your planned return date. If you are not a European Union citizen, check the visa requirements for the countries you will visit along the Rhine (Germany, France, the Netherlands, and Switzerland).

While not required, travel insurance is strongly advised. It provides peace of mind by offering cash protection in the event of unforeseen circumstances such as travel cancellation, medical problems, or misplaced luggage. Choose a plan that fits your requirements and budget.

Travel Documents: Keep copies of your cruise confirmation, airplane bookings, travel insurance policy, and any other important documents organized and easily accessible. Consider saving digital copies on your phone or in cloud storage for convenient retrieval.

Visa Requirements: Check visa requirements well in advance of your trip, especially if you're traveling from a nation that isn't part of the Schengen Area's visa-waiver program. Contact the embassies or consulates of the countries you intend to visit to find out whether a visa is required and how to apply.

Make copies of your passport's photo and information page and store them separate in case of loss or theft. Maintain a digital copy of your passport information in a secure location as well.

Packing the Essentials

Clothing

Pack for the season - layers are essential because the weather might be unpredictable. Light jackets and sweaters may be required in the spring and autumn, while breathable fabrics are recommended in the summer. Winter calls for warm clothing such as thermal layers, a coat, waterproof boots, a hat, and gloves.

Comfortable walking shoes are essential for exploring towns and villages. Pack sandals or lightweight shoes for warmer weather or resting on the deck.

Pack one dressier clothing for optional elegant evenings on the cruise ship or special dinners at posh restaurants on land.

Amenities: Bring any necessary amenities, such as sunscreen, bug repellant, hand sanitizer, and any prescriptions you need. Consider using travel-sized containers to save room. Remember that some toiletries may be available for purchase onboard at a premium, so plan accordingly.

Personal Items: Don't forget to bring a swimsuit for the pool or hot tub onboard, sunglasses, a hat, and a reusable water bottle to stay hydrated during your journey. If you are traveling from a nation that has a different electrical system, you will need an adaptor plug.

Check with your cruise line about laundry service availability onboard. Pack accordingly, knowing that you can refresh your clothes as needed.

Electronics and Gadgets

Smartphone: Your smartphone is a useful travel companion. Download vital apps for navigation, translation, currency conversion, and communication with loved ones back home. Ensure you have an international roaming plan, or consider getting a local SIM card upon arrival for more cost-effective data usage.

Camera: Photograph the breathtaking scenery, beautiful cities, and unforgettable experiences of your Rhine River Cruise. A high-quality camera with a zoom lens is desirable. Consider using a waterproof case for further protection, particularly on shore excursions.

Load your favorite books, periodicals, or movies onto an e-reader or tablet to keep you entertained during your cruise downtime.

Portable Charger: A portable charger guarantees that your devices remain charged throughout your journey, which is especially important for capturing those perfect vacation moments.

Download movies, audiobooks, or podcasts to your devices ahead of time for offline entertainment on aircraft or in areas with restricted Wi-Fi availability.

Safety Instruments

While the Rhine River Cruise is generally a safe experience, packing a few basic safety items can provide peace of mind.

First Aid Kit: A small first aid kit with basic materials like bandages, antiseptic wipes, painkillers, and medication for common illnesses like dyspepsia or allergies can be useful for minor wounds or medical emergencies.

Personal Locator Beacon (PLB): For daring travelers traveling off the usual path during shore excursions, a PLB can save their lives in the event of an emergency in isolated areas. A PLB sends a distress signal that can be detected by search and rescue personnel.

Door Security Wedge: A little door security wedge can give an extra layer of security to your cabin door, particularly for light sleepers or those looking for peace of mind.

Familiarize yourself with the safety features on your cruise ship. Locate the life vests, muster stations, and emergency exits. In the unusual case of an emergency, being cool and obeying crew instructions are critical.

By following these detailed instructions and packing essentials for paperwork, daily necessities, devices, and even optional safety measures, you'll be well-prepared to embark on your Rhine River Cruise with confidence and a sense of adventure. Set sail and prepare to make memories that will last a lifetime!

CHAPTER 8

Accommodation Option

The Rhine Valley offers a varied choice of hotel alternatives to suit a variety of tastes and budgets. This section digs into two common options: hotels and AirBnB rentals, to help you find the ideal home base for your Rhine River adventure.

Hotels

Hotels provide a conventional and handy option for your Rhine River vacation. Here's a breakdown of the benefits hotels offer:

There are hotels to suit every taste and budget, ranging from luxury five-star places to quaint boutique hotels and low-cost options.

Many hotels are located in the middle of picturesque towns and cities along the Rhine, providing convenient access to historical monuments, shops, and restaurants. Some hotels also have spectacular riverbank positions that provide visitors with stunning valley views.

Hotels often provide a variety of amenities and services to help you enjoy your stay. This could include comfy beds, daily housekeeping, on-site restaurants and bars, fitness centers, spas, and concierge services to help with tour reservations or restaurant recommendations.

All-Inclusive Packages: Some hotels have all-inclusive packages, which might be an economical option. These packages may include breakfast, supper, drinks, and even shore excursions on your Rhine River Cruise. This makes budgeting easier and allows you to focus on enjoying your vacation.

Hotel Coellner Hof

The majestic structure combines heritage and modernity in a harmonious way. Values, excellent comfort, and solid-earth quality all contribute to the house's personal touch and unique appeal. When you enter the lobby, you can experience a sense of well-being. Stylish and made from well selected materials, the guest areas have been rebuilt and reshaped over the previous few years to provide contemporary and sophisticated comfort to guests who would no longer overlook them. Whether traveling for business, as seminar participants, exhibitors, or guests, as tourists, or simply passing through, the "Coellner Hof" can apply to any fair claim. Located in the city center, just a few minutes' walk from Cologne Cathedral, Media Park, the Opera House, the Philharmonic Society, commercial streets, and the old town of Cologne. Lanxess Arena Cologne fair is conveniently located near our hotel "Coellner Court". Whether you're on a private or professional vacation, we're the right city hotel in Cologne.

Hyatt Regency Köln

The Hyatt Regency Cologne, with views of Cologne Cathedral, Old Town, and the Rhine River, is ideal for your trip to Cologne. Guests enjoy exclusive service, spacious accommodations, a fashionable atmosphere, a modern health facility with pool, and various cuisine. With a view of the Rhine, you can enjoy the best international cuisine, elegant cocktails, Italian specialties, and unique street food delicacies.

Adina Apartment Hotel Cologne

The Adina Hotel Cologne is conveniently located on the "West 4", immediately between the Cologne trade fair "koelnmesse" with its massive meeting center and the Messe/Deutz rail station. The old town, including Cologne Cathedral, is only a 15-minute walk away, and a neighboring train station provides excellent connections to the city center and other long-distance and local excursions.

Steigenberger Hotel Koln

The landmarked Steigenberger Hotel Köln lies in the heart of the city, within a few minutes' walk from major historical attractions. The 305 modern rooms, some with stunning views of the iconic Cologne Cathedral, have comfortable equipment, modern decor, and pleasant colors that invite you to unwind after a long day. Air conditioning, television, a telephone with free local calls, a work desk, a safe, a minibar, and coffee and tea making facilities are among the amenities. After around 20 minutes of walking, you'll arrive at the world-famous Cologne Cathedral and the Rhine promenade. Visit the Gothic cathedral and walk through the ancient district's twisting passageways. Take a break with a refreshing Kölsch beer from one of the many taverns and rustic breweries that line the "Alter Markt" square. More distant locations, as well as the Cologne Trade Fair, are easily accessible by public transportation from the hotel's "Rudolfplatz".

Choosing The Right Hotel

Consider your budget. Hotels vary in price based on location, facilities, and star rating. Determine your budget and select a hotel that provides the degree of comfort and services you seek within your budget.

Location is key: Consider your intended degree of activity. If you intend to spend most of your time exploring towns and cities, a central location is best. Consider hotels in tiny villages or on the outskirts, which provide a more serene environment.

Amenities matter: Prioritize the amenities that are most important to you. Do you need a fitness center or a spa? Is on-site eating important to you, or do you prefer to explore local restaurants? Choosing a hotel that has the amenities you will need ensures a more enjoyable stay.

AirBnB

AirBnB rentals have become a popular choice for travelers looking for a unique and local experience. Here's an overview of what AirBnB offers:

Unique Stays: AirBnB provides a wide choice of rentals, from exquisite flats in ancient buildings to quaint cottages set among vineyards. This allows you to have a more personal experience with the local culture and architecture than a standard hotel room.

Local Flavor: AirBnB homes are frequently owned and maintained by locals, allowing you to interact with the community and learn about their way of life. Some hosts may even identify hidden treasures or local restaurants that are off the beaten route.

Flexibility and Space: AirBnB rentals, particularly apartments or houses, can provide greater space than traditional hotel rooms. This is perfect for families or parties vacationing together, as it provides more privacy and a sense of home away from home. Some rentals may include kitchens or kitchenettes, allowing you to cook your own meals or enjoy leisurely breakfasts at your own speed.

Things to Consider with AirBnB

Location: Some AirBnBs may be centrally placed, while others may be in more tranquil regions. When selecting a rental, consider your desired closeness to town centers and attractions.

Before reserving an AirBnB, carefully read the reviews and ratings left by previous guests. This can provide valuable information on the property's condition, amenities, location, and the host's communication style.

Communicate clearly with your host prior to your arrival. Discuss the check-in procedures, amenities provided, and any house regulations that may apply.

Finally, the greatest Rhine River Cruise accommodations will depend on your own interests and travel style. Hotels provide a convenient and hassle-free experience with a variety of features. AirBnB rentals offer a distinct and local flavor, potentially providing additional space and flexibility. Weigh the advantages and disadvantages of each option to find the ideal place to relax and recharge after a day of seeing the gorgeous Rhine Valley.

CHAPTER 9

Outdoor Adventure and Activities

The Rhine Valley is more than just attractive towns and magnificent castles. It's a haven for outdoor enthusiasts, with a wide selection of activities to let you reconnect with nature and enjoy the region's spectacular scenery. This section showcases exciting choices for individuals looking for adventure and fresh air on their Rhine River cruise.

Beaches and Coastal Escapes

While the Rhine is not known for its typical beaches, your cruise itinerary may include a stop in the Netherlands, where you can experience the seaside.

Dutch Delights: If your Rhine River Cruise includes a stop in the Netherlands, take in the country's breathtaking coastline. Relax on the sandy beaches of Scheveningen, a beautiful coastal resort town located near The Hague. Stretch out on a sun lounger, enjoy a cool dip in the North Sea, or wander down the picturesque seafront lined with quaint cafés and restaurants.

Island hopping: For an unforgettable coastal trip, visit the Dutch Wadden Islands. These islands, which are accessible by ferry from the mainland, include pristine beaches, car-free settlements, and plenty of opportunity for animal watching. Explore the natural splendor of Texel National Park or ride a bike over the dunes of Schiermonnikoog, a car-free island noted for its pristine scenery.

If your schedule involves a visit on the Dutch coast, bring a swimsuit and a beach towel. On a hot summer day, the North Sea's refreshing waters can provide a welcome break.

Hiking and Natural Trails

The Rhine Valley is crisscrossed by well-maintained hiking routes that cater to hikers of all skill levels.

Rheinsteig Trail: The Rheinsteig Trail, a 310-kilometer (193-mile) long-distance trail that runs from Wiesbaden to Bonn, is a difficult but rewarding journey for experienced hikers. The walk provides breathtaking panoramic views of the river valley, picturesque villages, and medieval castles.

The Mittelrhein Klettersteig is a difficult via ferrata trail near the Loreley Rock formation that thrill-seekers can take on. This fixed-cable climbing route demands a mind for heights and the necessary equipment, but it rewards participants with stunning views and an adrenaline rush.

Vineyard Walks: For a more leisurely experience, follow the network of trails that loop through the vineyards that cover the hills beside the Rhine. These leisurely walks allow you to immerse yourself in the region's renowned wine culture, observe the stunning surroundings, and possibly stop at a winery for a sampling session.

Purchase a hiking map of the area or download a hiking app to identify paths that suit your fitness level and interests. Many towns and villages provide guided hikes led by informed locals.

Water Sports and Adventures Tourism

The Rhine River itself provides a playground for water-related activities.

Cycling and E-biking: The Rhine Cycle Path is a picturesque path that runs along the river for nearly 1,200 kilometers (745 miles). Explore the riverbanks at your leisure, pausing to visit picturesque towns and villages along the route.

E-bikes are a popular choice for individuals who want a less demanding method to tour the route.

Kayaking and canoeing: For a unique view of the Rhine Valley, explore the river in a kayak or canoe. Paddle by vineyards, picturesque villages, and historic castles, taking in the peacefulness and natural beauty of the area. Guided kayaking trips are provided for individuals looking for a safe and educational experience.

River Cruises: While your main Rhine River Cruise is a comfortable way to see the region, look into shorter river cruises offered by local firms. These cruises may concentrate on certain sections of the river, providing a more intimate experience and the opportunity to discover secret coves and inlets.

Several firms provide bicycle rentals and guided cycling tours along the Rhine. Kayak and canoe rentals are also offered in several communities along the river. Before participating in any water-based activities, make sure to check the weather and water levels.

By getting off the cruise ship and enjoying the outdoors, you'll have a better appreciation for the

Rhine Valley's natural beauty and different landscapes. So lace up your hiking boots, grab your paddle, or hop on a bike and prepare to experience the Rhine's charm from a completely new perspective!

CHAPTER 10

Sustainability and Responsible Tourism

The Rhine River is a rich source of cultural history and natural beauty. As responsible travelers, we share a joint obligation to ensure its preservation for future generations. This section discusses sustainable practices and responsible tourism recommendations for reducing your environmental effect and supporting local communities on your Rhine River Cruise.

Eco - Friendly Practices

Embrace Reusable Items: Packing a reusable water bottle, shopping bags, and coffee cup helps to reduce single-use plastics. Many cafes and restaurants provide discounts for using your own mug, allowing you to enjoy your morning coffee while reducing waste.

Minimize Energy Consumption: Be conscious of how much energy you use in your cabin. Turn off lights and electronics when not in use, and consider participating in towel reuse programs offered by some cruise lines. Take shorter showers to save water.

Pack light and choose environmentally friendly products: Choose travel-sized toiletries and environmentally friendly choices whenever possible. Look for products that have minimum packaging or are manufactured from recycled materials. Packing light also lowers your cruise ship's fuel use.

Respect wildlife: The Rhine River is home to a variety of animals, including birds, fish, and otters. Admire these creatures from a respectful distance and don't harm their habitats. If you go on a wildlife watching excursion, consider providers who are committed to sustainable techniques.

Several cruise companies are actively developing environmentally friendly methods, such as using biofuels, minimizing waste generation, and investing in renewable energy. When booking a cruise, consider investigating cruise lines with strong sustainability programs.

Supporting Local Communities

Shop Local and Support Artisans: Rather than massive chain stores, look for local shops and marketplaces that provide handcrafted souvenirs and regional products. This puts money directly into the local economy and helps craftsmen retain traditional crafts.

Dine at Local Restaurants: Look beyond the cruise ship buffets and try some local restaurants. This allows you to sample authentic regional cuisine, support local companies, and engage with the community.

Choose Local Guides: When scheduling tours or excursions, think about hiring local guides. They provide significant insights into the region's history, culture, and hidden gems, and their profits directly support the community.

Respect Local Customs and Traditions: When visiting religious sites, dress modestly and stay aware of local customs and traditions. Learning a few basic phrases in German (or French/Dutch if your cruise goes beyond Germany) shows respect and appreciation for the local culture.

Many towns and villages along the Rhine provide walking excursions led by enthusiastic locals. These tours offer a distinct perspective on the region's history and culture, frequently deviating from the conventional tourist route.

Responsible Travel Tips

Minimize trash and recycle appropriately. Use the recycling containers supplied on board the cruise ship and in public areas during shore excursions. When exploring natural regions, don't trash and leave no trace.

Be Mindful of Water usage: While staying hydrated is important, be mindful of water usage, especially in locations where water is scarce. Choose to refill your reusable water bottle rather than purchasing new plastic ones at every opportunity.

Protect the Natural Environment: Show respect for the Rhine's vulnerable ecosystems. Hike on designated routes, avoid collecting wildflowers, and don't damage wildlife habitats.

Support Sustainable firms: When selecting hotels, restaurants, or activity providers, choose firms who are committed to sustainable practices. Look for eco-certifications or ask about their environmental initiatives.

Pack a small bag on shore trips to avoid collecting plastic shopping bags. This enables you to transport products from local stores or markets without generating unneeded garbage.

By embracing these practices and adopting a responsible travel mindset, you can ensure that your Rhine River Cruise has a good environmental impact while also supporting the local populations that live in this intriguing region. Together, we can conserve the Rhine's charm for future generations to discover and enjoy.

CONCLUSION

The Rhine River, a gleaming ribbon of history and spectacular beauty, awaits your discovery. This intriguing river promises an amazing tour through lovely villages, stunning castles, and breathtaking scenery.

Allow the enchantment of the Rhine River Cruise to sweep you away. Immerse yourself in the rich fabric of history, experience the wonderful cuisine, and get enchanted by the Rhine Valley. From visiting ancient Roman ruins to indulging in world-class wines, each bend in the river reveals a new treasure waiting to be uncovered.

This guide has been your travel companion, providing you with the knowledge and motivation to embark on a memorable experience. Remember, the Rhine experience goes beyond the perfectly planned agenda. Take advantage of the opportunity to get off the main route, meet people, and make memories that will last a lifetime.

Our heartfelt gratitude goes out to you, the traveler. Your curiosity and eagerness to discover fuel our enthusiasm for creating unforgettable travel experiences. We really hope that this book has given you the courage to sail the Rhine, make memorable experiences, and embrace the beauty that awaits along this intriguing waterway.

May your journey be full of surprise, discovery, and a strong connection to the wonderful Rhine Valley.

Printed in Great Britain
by Amazon